Growth

God's Extraordinary Lessons
from Ordinary Occurrences

Janice M. Allen

Allen Creative Group
Ridgecrest, California

Scripture quotations marked AMP have been taken from the Amplified® Bible (AMP), Copyright © 2015 by The Lockman Foundation. Used by permission. www.lockman.org.
Scripture quotations marked CSB have been taken from the Christian

♦ DEDICATION ♦

To my wonderful husband, Pastor Sammie L. Allen, Sr.
To my beloved mom, Mary A. McCoy.
To the true author of this book,
my Lord and Savior, Jesus Christ.

♦ FOREWORD BY STEPHANIE M. FREEMAN ♦

"Balloons contain a thousand breaths, and a million prayers more. One thing is sure in a world that is not: His Love never changes. She basks in the light of His salvation and holds her prayers high. Miles beyond the edge of faith, she continues to grow and learn. His love surrounds her. Living water sustains her through the droughts and famines of the soul. His word is the lullaby of the ages and a map for the lost still searching for home."

Stephanie M. Freeman
Author of *Necessary Evil* and *Unfinished Business*

♦ FOREWORD BY PASTOR SAMMIE ALLEN, SR. ♦

"*GROWTH* is inspirational, instructional, and educational as it relates real-life situations and experiences to the Word of God. It leaves the reader smiling, encouraged, and motivated to overcome obstacles and grow in their relationship with Jesus Christ. I praise the Lord for gifting me with His true servant, Janice M. Allen, who pours herself into ensuring that His readers have received 'God's Extraordinary Lessons from Ordinary Occurrences.' I believe this is the most inspirational book of the year."

Pastor Sammie L. Allen, Sr.
Senior Pastor, New Beginnings Baptist Fellowship (Ridgecrest, CA)

◆ FOREWORD BY PASTOR DAN WILLIS ◆

"Janice M. Allen is the absolute most prolific writer and author I have personally known in 43 years pastoring The Lighthouse Church of All Nations in Chicago, IL. Her skill, knowledge and warmth leaves the reader with something glowing in their soul, never to be forgotten. Everyone who has ever experienced scars, abuse, injustice, or spiritual injury MUST read this book! Through the lens of someone who is so very loving to everyone she comes in contact with, you will begin to understand the answers to life's questions you have struggled with.

The content has been laboriously studied, prayed over, and edited by trustworthy Men and Women of God. This allows you to know that truly the scripture has been fulfilled as you read this book.

Proverbs 11:14 states this: *"... in the multitude of counsellors there is safety."* I HIGHLY recommend this amazing book to you, dear friends.

Your life will be so BLESSED as you feast at this table."

Pastor Dan Willis
Senior Pastor, The Lighthouse Church of All Nations (Chicago, IL)

♦ ACKNOWLEDGEMENTS ♦

"I love when people that have been through hell walk out of the flames carrying buckets of water for those still consumed by the fire." (Stephanie Sparkles)

Who goes through life without bruises and knockdowns? No one. But do you know who comes out on the other side with healing and strength? Those who make up in their minds that they want a different way of experiencing life. The good news is that there's no reason why you can't be that person.

As you read the experiences shared in this book, I pray that you will be strengthened to grow into all that the Lord Jesus has purposed you to be. May this book prompt you to look at your own life and see that the hand of God is at work on your behalf, through the good and not so good times. I pray that the words on these pages will embolden you to confront your fears, your feelings of inadequacy, your inability to value yourself, and whatever else is holding you back, for these roadblocks can be conquered through the knowledge that God has a good plan for you.

James Blanchard Cisneros said, "Your healing and growth are an example to many.... For in you, they will see themselves. In your victory, they will find their hope."

So, my friend, as I offer a little of myself to you through this book, I thank God in advance for the laughter, contemplation, and healing it will bring.

Stay blessed. Stay encouraged. Stay strengthened.

I can't end my acknowledgements without giving my heartfelt thanks to those who helped bring this book to fruition.

To my husband, Pastor Sammie L. Allen, Sr.: I love you. You'll never know how much I cherish your undying support. You are the sunshine that makes me blossom. I am forever grateful that God brought us together.

To my mom, Mary McCoy: I couldn't have become the woman I am without your loving and nurturing presence in my life. You mean the world to me.

To Naleighna Kai: Thank you for being such a wonderful friend. You're one of a kind. The mentoring you give me and others is priceless. Thank you for allowing me to be part of Naleighna Kai's Tribe Called Success. And thank you for your editing expertise.

To J. L. Campbell: You are a jewel in the world of editing. Thank you for polishing my diamond.

To Debra Mitchell: You are the best beta reader everrrr!

To J. L. Woodson: Nobody can create magnificent book covers like you can. I'm forever grateful for your talent.

To Shawn Williams, thank you for providing Naleighna Kai with that nudge!

To Naleighna Kai's Tribe Called Success: I love every one of you.

Janice M. Allen

Penny Silly

LIFE EXPERIENCE:

When I was growing up, my grandmother used to give me and my two younger cousins chewable orange baby aspirin every day in the wintertime. This ritual prevented us from getting sore throats or fevers. The very first time she doled out the little pills, my cousins Debra and Dawanna obediently chewed theirs. I, on the other hand, didn't like that bitter orange taste and chalky texture. I told my grandmother as much.

"Chew it up," she replied. "It tastes like candy."

The nasty little thing had already melted in my mouth anyway, so I choked it down my throat. Then I set my five-year-old mind to planning how to avoid taking another one.

When she gave me a baby aspirin the next day, I slyly dropped it in the water while washing my hands. Splashing the water around a little made the small pill dissolve, and no one was the wiser. I was the brightest five-year-old I knew, outsmarting my grandmother and all. In reality, I was the only five-year-old I knew, but that's beside the point.

For a couple of days I did that disappearing trick. On day three, however, I developed a sore throat. My two cousins stayed healthy, while my ailment progressed into chronically swollen tonsils that home remedies couldn't heal. My grandparents had to take me to the doctor, and that was back in the days when folks cured everything at home.

At the clinic, Dr. Knight sat me on the examining table, put that 'popsicle stick' on my tongue, and aimed a miniature flashlight at the back of my throat. One moment, I felt weak and hot, then cold and sweaty the next. It hurt when I swallowed.

Putting down his instruments and feeling my neck, he said to the nurse, "Yeah, we need to give her a shot of penicillin."

Two of his words stood out to me. 'Penicillin' because it sounded like 'penny silly,' which would have been quite comical to my little ears had I not been so sick. I also heard the word 'shot'. That wasn't funny at all because I'd been down that road a time or two and knew some pain was in my near future.

I pleaded for my grandparents to get me out of there. You've never seen a thirty-pound human fight so hard. It took both of them plus the nurse to hold me down so the doctor could administer the shot.

Once we got back home, I showed my cousins the bandage over my injection site, and with a pitiful face told them all about the doctor giving me a shot of 'penny silly.'

GROWTH:

At the time, I was too young to know that this great pain could have been avoided had I endured the lesser unpleasantness of taking that baby aspirin for a little while.

Looking back, many bitter pills—in the form of pains, hardships, challenges, and heartaches—have come my way in sixty years of living. I can't lie; I spent a lot of time trying to make every one of them vanish. Unfortunately, suffering and trials don't melt away as easily as my baby aspirin did. There have been situations that did not go away when I prayed, no matter how fervently I expressed to God what I wanted. There have been ordeals that did not end when I commanded them to, no matter how much scripture I quoted.

The reality is that no one is going to live on this earth without some anguish and difficulty. Thankfully, God has a way of causing even our distress to benefit us—if we let Him. Hear what God says.

> *"I say this because I know what I am planning for you," says the Lord. "I have good plans for you, not plans to hurt you. I will give you hope and a good future"* (Jeremiah 29:11 NCV).

God does not necessarily cause every dilemma that comes into our lives, but He can certainly use them to make us stronger. He says that He declares the end from the beginning (Isaiah 46:10). That means that before things happen in our lives, God already knows the outcome. And why should this be so difficult to believe? My grandmother was not God, yet she could foresee the end (my great sickness) that would inevitably spring from the beginning (my sore throat and fever). Though she didn't cause it, she certainly saw it coming. How much greater is God's foresight?

Nevertheless, at the ripe old age of five, I discarded my grandmother's insight and relied on my little bit of "wisdom". In the end, I learned two things. (1) What she had said was correct (take the baby aspirin so you won't get sick). (2) She was concerned about what's best for me.

Those two things apply just as much to God. Everything He says is true and He looks out for my best interest without any speculation or guesswork. As Jeremiah 29:11 makes plain, He knows what He's doing. But how often in my adult life have I let a detestable situation get the best of me because I put trust in my instincts instead of in the omniscient God who knows everything about my circumstance? He promises that He has plans to take care of me. So the question is—will I trust Him? When I'm in a predicament, will I trust the infinite knowledge of the God who knows what He is doing and has it all planned out? Or will I trust my own limited knowledge and beg and plead for Him to make the bitter pill go away? Will I allow God to do what my grandmother tried to do: use something disagreeable to strengthen me to fight off a coming calamity?

Think of it this way: while you're busy asking God to change the situation, God is busy asking you to let Him use the situation to change you; to make you stronger; to mature you as a Christian.

The Lifter Up of My Head

LIFE EXPERIENCE:

You and I know that it is highly unfair and downright wrong for a middle-aged woman to have to deal with wrinkles and pimples on her face at the same time. For decades, I used every concoction on the market that said I could eliminate acne by getting rid of my skin's excess oil. Unbeknownst to me, these remedies were so harsh and drying that they set the stage for premature wrinkles. When wrinkles emerged, I bought other potions that promised to restore my youthful skin. How was I to know that they would overload my pores with oil, causing huge blackheads to flourish? I was stuck in a vicious cycle. Zap the zits, cultivate more creases. Wallop the wrinkles, activate the acne.

No worries; I found the perfect solution.

A facelift. That's what I needed. It would make me pretty and pull me out of the funk that had become my very own midlife crisis. And although the crisis I was experiencing was internal, I thought the cause—and thus the solution—were to be found externally.

At the time, I was forty-six. Granted, I was no spring chicken. However, I felt that the untimely aging of my skin made me look like a *really old hen.* I became more and more discontent with my appearance. Each time I looked in a mirror, my eyes attacked my face, scanning the uneven texture of my skin and critically assessing the too-large pores.

Again and again, my gaze roamed across the rough facial landscape that had been created by years of acne scars, looking for something delicate, something feminine, some prettiness in this face of mine.

I got a shocker one day when I pulled out my driver's license and noticed how much my face had aged in the four years since I had posed for that photo. The me on the driver's license had a beautiful smile, a slim face with firm, tight skin draped over a pleasing bone structure. The reflection in the looking glass had a countenance that was drawn, hollowed out, and worn. The smile wasn't even the same on this used-up face. I didn't see the beauty and joy I wanted to project; just a sad, old, droopy face that was telling all my secrets. Like a billboard advertising the pains I worked so hard to hide, it told any and everyone who would listen that life had taken me through the wringer more than a few times.

Well, since my face wanted to betray me, I was going to show it who was boss. Yes indeed, a facelift would teach it a thing or two. Besides, in this day and age, it was as common as going to get your hair done, I reasoned to myself.

I began researching different facial rejuvenation techniques and settled on one that was supposed to be less invasive. But after the procedure was finished and the swelling went down, that old familiar feeling began to show up again—the feeling that I didn't like how I looked.

That made me even more self-conscious. Over time, even my posture reflected how displeased I was with myself. At 5'9", I should have been statuesque, standing tall and majestic. But because I didn't like what I saw, I was eager to fade into the background. I walked around with my shoulders hunched and head bowed, avoiding eye contact as much as possible to subconsciously make myself unnoticeable.

Although the doctor gave my face an overhaul, it was hard to admit that I had not found contentment. Looking at someone else's life helped me understand the nature of my real problem.

I once worked with a guy who always juggled two or three girlfriends at a time. Sometimes, the strain of keeping multiple girlfriends blissfully unaware of each other stressed him out. When he reached that point, he'd create an elaborate plan to redecorate a part of his home. He'd choose a room, do an extensive makeover that rivaled an HGTV dream home, then bring before-and-after pictures to show his coworkers. How easy it had been for him to fall into the belief that *outside* changes would remedy his *inside* turmoil.

That was akin to my facelift experience. I did some rearranging, but I didn't address the underlying problem. See, the challenge wasn't loose facial muscles or loss of elasticity in my skin. The underlying problem was the inner pain I refused to deal with.

GROWTH:

The doctor had lifted the sagging skin on my face. Yet he was ill-equipped to lift the veil of heaviness, sadness, and dissatisfaction I had been struggling with. He prescribed painkillers to help me manage the discomfort associated with the procedure, but he couldn't give me anything to help manage the emotional pain I was running from.

The lesson I learned was that while I was running around looking for someone to lift my face, all I really needed was the One who could lift my head.

> But thou, O LORD, art a shield for me; my glory, and the lifter up of mine head (Psalm 3:3 KJV).

God began a work of healing in my heart when I read that scripture and allowed it to take root inside me. He whispered that only He knew my real pains. Even I didn't know them all because I consistently chose to bury them. Then, He whispered a most important secret. He made me know that in Him I could find healing from my pain, restoration from my brokenness.

So many women today are experiencing the same sort of challenges that I faced. They believe they're too heavy or too skinny. Their noses are too broad, their hair too thin. We zero in on our flaws because we are unaware—or have forgotten—that we are made in the image and likeness of God (Genesis 1:27). In fact, Psalm 139:14 says we are *"fearfully and wonderfully made"* (KJV).

Changing how I see my outer appearance wasn't something that happened overnight. It took time and a willingness on my part to re¬shape what I think of myself by looking through His loving eyes instead of through my own hyper-critical ones. As I learned to value and love who I am, I automatically started liking my looks.

God didn't change my appearance. Instead, He gave me a new perspective about my looks. And that, my friend, is absolutely, positively … beautiful.

Fear Not

LIFE EXPERIENCE:

I don't like snakes. Big or small, real or fake, if it's a snake, *I don't like it*. I'm terrified of them. The way they skulk along the ground, quiet as a ninja, turns my stomach. If I stumble upon one as I flip through the television channels, I snap my head away from the screen, leave the room, or change the channel—anything to make it go away. Just typing the word 'snake' right now is making my skin crawl.

You would think that I wouldn't get so disturbed by them, considering that I lived in a place called Roe, Arkansas, for the first five years of my life. The population at that time was under 100 people, but there were countless creepy serpents around. It didn't matter if they were rattlers or harmless garter snakes, I never overcame my fear of them. On numerous occasions my grandmother fought off snakes with a fishing pole, a garden hoe, or whatever she happened to have in her hand at the time. Evidently, I took after my grandfather's side of the family. As the story goes, one of his nephews donned hunting gear one morning and headed toward the woods to track deer, only to trudge right back in the door minutes later, rifle in hand, visibly shaken because he had come within inches of stepping on a snake. Yes indeed, friends, snake-hatin' is in my blood.

So why in the wee hours of a January morning in 2008 did I have this strange dream about a snake? As I slumbered, I saw myself in a wheat field. The wheat was tall, maybe a little more than waist high. And slithering through those blond shafts of grain was a gigantic snake, bigger than an anaconda. This mustard-colored thing was moving fast, creating a ripple through the stalks, not unlike the wavy trail a speedboat leaves as it zips through the water. And it was coming straight for me.

Knowing what you know about me, you already figured out that my first inclination was to haul booty and run for dear life. And I did run, but not as you might expect. I didn't turn my back on the coming terror. Instead, I ran *backward*, moving away from the serpent while at the same time keeping an eye on it to know exactly where it was.

When that sinister creature got close enough to touch me, I abruptly stopped and looked right at it. The snake instantly came to a standstill, its coiled body towering over me. I didn't cower, cover my eyes, cry, or even have a sudden need for Depends. I kept my eyes fixed on the snake because it was clear that it intended to strike. However, it couldn't attack, though it desperately wanted to.

After the third or fourth time that it drew itself into battle stance and bared its deadly fangs, I shouted at it. No intelligible words. No scripture that I had memorized. Only a loud, sharp yell flew from my mouth. And wonder of all wonders, at the sound of my voice, this scaly tormentor *deflated* like a balloon with a giant pinhole. In the blink of an eye, it lost all its power.

GROWTH:

What scares you? What thing in your life immobilizes you with fear? Fear that you won't be able to make it through this pandemic? Fear that just one more thing stressing you out will send you over the edge? Fear of death? Fear of failure? Fear of success?

The snake represented the many fears that limited me and held me back for most of my life. But unlike in real life, the fear in my dream wasn't able to sneak up and catch me by surprise. That trickster wasn't so slick, after all; it left tracks in the wheat. I saw its every move.

That brings to mind what Paul said in 2 Corinthians 2:11. There he tells us that we are not ignorant of Satan's devices. One of Satan's greatest weapons is fear. It has often worked on me, immobilizing, paralyzing, and terrorizing me. Not this time. Not in this dream. As the enemy came out for the chase, I never turned my back on him. Instead, I kept the snake firmly within my sights. Although running forward would have increased my speed and decreased my chances of falling, I kept running backward, never taking my eyes off the enemy.

Each time it stopped and positioned itself to strike, I held my ground and looked right at it. And although its intent was certainly clear, it was as though I had an invisible force field that wouldn't allow it to boldly go where no snake had gone before. (Yes, I took that one from Star Trek).

What happened in my dream was exactly like what the Bible describes in Isaiah 59:19.

... When the enemy comes in like a flood, the Spirit of the LORD will lift up a standard against him (NKJV).

It wasn't my presence that stopped the serpent. The presence of the Spirit of the Lord did that. On the snake's last attempt to pounce, my voice rendered him powerless. That troublemaker heard my voice, but it was the power of God in me that made it respond as it did.

Your snake might be the two-legged kind: family, friends, co¬workers, etc. Your snake may be a financial crisis that has you answering the phone and saying in a fake accent "She no live here!" when you discover it's a bill collector on the line. Or it may come in the form of a pink slip from your employer. Perhaps it's the fear that you or someone you love will meet their demise by COVID-19. Regardless, look to God for your strength.

God is our refuge and strength, a very present help in trouble. Therefore we will not fear... (Psalm 46:1-2 NKJV).

Fishers of Men

During my thirty years of working as a legal secretary in downtown Chicago, I passed a lot of homeless people on the sidewalk. Sometimes I gave someone a donation. At other times I didn't offer money, either because I didn't have change, or I had it but didn't feel safe offering it to that particular person. The one thing I did have to offer everyday was my smile and a kind word. And it seems like many of them cherished this as much as money because it meant that someone saw value in them, saw them as a fellow human worthy of even casual interaction.

I formed a special bond with one lady I'll call Sylvie. She lived in a shelter and made her living selling Streetwise magazine. The founder of Streetwise created it to give homeless people a chance to help themselves by selling a newspaper to earn an income instead of having to beg on the streets.

Thursday was the day Sylvie would sell her magazines on the corner where my office building was located. Despite her situation, she always tried to remain positive. I looked forward to seeing her each week.

One day I asked her if she believed that God loved her and had a good plan for her life. She was honest enough to say she wanted to believe, but sometimes it was a stretch. I told her about my church and said if she ever wanted to visit, she could call me and I'd pick her up.

So I wasn't surprised when I stopped to talk with her one fall day and she told me that the previous weekend, she had visited a church that was within walking distance of her homeless shelter. The elation I felt over hearing that she had gone was snatched away when she relayed what she had experienced.

"It was a huge church," she said. "I walked down the middle aisle, hoping to blend in with the other people looking for seats, but knowing I couldn't. My dress was second-hand and kinda short. Not mini-skirt short. Just … short. I did wear leggings underneath to make myself more presentable. Even though they had a couple small holes, they helped me expose a little less skin."

She stopped to greet someone who came up to purchase a newspaper from her. Then she turned back to our conversation.

"Living out of a homeless shelter doesn't leave me many wardrobe choices. A person just has to make the best out of whatever they can get their hands on." Her eyes clouded as she added, "Compared to the fancy hats, expensive suits, and designer shoes on the people around me, I felt like a Yugo in a Rolls Royce showroom."

Sylvie told me how she'd spotted an empty seat in the third row from the back and hurried over, hoping no one else would take it before she got there. The man and woman on the end of that row were standing with hands raised and eyes closed as they swayed to a melody coming from the choir. She timidly touched the woman's arm and pointed to the empty seat. The woman gave her a warm smile then tapped the man's shoulder before stepping into the aisle to let Sylvie by.

The man eyed his wife, not even trying to hide how aggravated he was at being disturbed during his worship experience. Looking Sylvie up and down with contempt, he muttered "Shoulda got here on time," then sat, leaving her just enough room to squeeze by without stepping on his feet or banging into his knees.

Shaking her head, she added, "There was a Bible on the empty seat. I asked if it was his, and he rolled his eyes like he couldn't believe I had the nerve to ask him to move it so I could sit."

I apologized to my friend for the horrible experience she had. I tried to assure her that not all people in church were like that.

"That's good to know," she said. "I tuned him out as best I could because I really went there seeking God. And the sermon the pastor preached was just what I needed to hear. When he ended it by saying that anyone who wanted to repent and dedicate themselves to the Lord could come to the altar for prayer, I stood and asked the man to let me by. At least he did stand up and move into the aisle this time so I could get past him. But as I got close to the aisle, he smirked and said, 'I bet you've got a whole lot to repent for, don't you?'"

With tears in her eyes, she asked me, "Why in the world would I want to be a Christian if this is the way they act?"

GROWTH:

A judgmental 'holier than thou' attitude is a killer. This mindset can smother a seed of faith that's been planted in a new believer. Not only that, it stifles the relationship between God and the prideful 'holier than thou' person because God resists the proud (1 Peter 5:5).

In Matthew 4:18-22, Jesus was walking by the sea of Galilee and saw four men who were fishermen. He said to them:

"Follow me, and I will make you fishers of men" (Matthew 4:19 NKJV).

Now if you've ever been fishing, you know that fish aren't 'skillet ready' when they come off the hook. After you catch them, they have to be prepped before you cook them. Prepping includes scraping the scales off the fish, slicing them open to remove their organs, deboning them, and cutting the meat into steaks or fillets. It would be ridiculous to get in a commercial fishing boat, catch hundreds of freshwater perch, then throw each one back because they were not already prepped when you hauled them out of the water.

As fishers of men, we are to bring people to Christ. Love them. Teach them. Disciple them. But leave the cleaning to God. He alone has the power to cleanse us from sin. Think of it this way: when we clean a fish, we kill it in the process. When God cleanses a person, He gives him or her new and eternal life.

The man in Sylvie's story judged her based on appearance only, and found her lacking because she didn't meet his standard of holiness. He made it clear that she would never be a 'good upstanding Christian' like him. The church was no place for someone like her. But having that man's mindset is dangerous. Jesus said,,

---

"Woe to the world because of the things that cause people to stumble! Such things must come, but woe to the person through whom they come!" (Matthew 18:7 NIV)

Great sorrow and distress will come to those who cause others to stumble. Believers are not to disparage or discourage others from coming to Christ. With open arms, open hearts, and open minds, we are to welcome the lost into the fold.

We catch 'em. God cleans 'em.

Don't Forget to Remember

LIFE EXPERIENCE:

Playing solitaire on my laptop or cell phone is one of my guilty pleasures. I win more than I lose. But that's only because after conquering the first three levels of difficulty, I tested the waters in the fourth level and kept getting outsmarted by the game. So instead of taking on the challenge and moving up the ranks through the remaining three levels of difficulty, I demoted myself to the medium level, where I am almost always a winner. Don't judge me. When I play solitaire, I'm looking for a fun outlet, not a way to stress myself out. So I stacked the deck in my favor by sticking to the easier games. And now I constantly experience the exhilaration that comes when the cards dance across the screen and the device plays a cute little tune in celebration of my win.

Now that I've gotten that confession out of the way, I can go on with the story. I sometimes run into a game that ends with the message "There are no more moves you can make." That means the game ended in a draw. My choices are to either replay that hand and try to get a win, or take the loss and play a new hand. I always replay the previous hand because at the elementary level I play in, none of the games are unsolvable.

What spurred this chapter is the fact that I just finished winning a game of solitaire—but it took me four tries to win that hand. I started it a couple days ago and it ended in a draw. I replayed the hand but didn't finish my second try because something important came up. Then, I went back to it yesterday and it ended in another draw. So I tackled that hand again today, knowing that the reason I kept losing was because I kept making the same moves. This time, I focused on what I could do differently. And on the fourth try, I won that hand.

GROWTH:

Here's the trick to replaying the hand of solitaire—you can't repeat previous moves and expect a different outcome. In other words, you can't win unless you remember what move caused you to fail and use that as a lesson on how to change your approach this time around.

Real life is no different. We sometimes hate the hand we're playing but we're unwilling to change anything. As much as we despise our dysfunction and want a better life, we linger in our defective state because at least we know what to expect from it. We're afraid to face the unknown that comes with stepping out of our comfort zone and doing something out of the norm.

Author John C. Maxwell wrote "The difference between where we are and where we want to be is created by the changes we are willing to make in our lives. When you want something you have never had, you must do something you've never done to get it. Otherwise, you keep getting the same results."

The Bible expresses the same sentiment when it says,

... *a fool repeats his foolishness* (Proverbs 26:11 CSB).

God is not saying that you're a horrible person if you make mistakes. But that verse points out how sad it is when a person makes the same mistake over and over again. As someone once penned, "Mistakes are meant for learning, not repeating." Our loving Father doesn't want us to spend time despairing over our mistakes. That only immobilizes us and bogs us down with guilt and condemnation. What God does want is for us to learn the lessons imbedded in our mistakes and grow from them. When the Israelites (His chosen people) spent forty years trying to reach a destination that only should have taken eleven days to get to, He said to them,

---

"...You've been going around in circles in these hills long enough; go north" (Deuteronomy 2:3 MSG).

So when you get tired of your life going in circles, seek God for direction. Ask Him what you should be doing differently. And then, do what He says.

Faith

LIFE EXPERIENCE:

Recently, I began exercising, and I hate it. Over the course of my life, I have found every excuse *not* to exercise: I have asthma; I hate sweating; it's hard finding time to exercise; exercising makes me hungry, then I eat more, and *gain* weight.

There's probably not an excuse out there that I haven't used, even though I know I can't develop a fit body without going through the discomfort of exercise. Yet, I have the nerve to step on the scale every morning God sends, hoping that the number has gone down from the day before, whether or not I've exercised.

And as comical as that is, the sad fact is that so many Christians operate in that mindset when it comes to our faith. We don't want to go through anything uncomfortable or challenging—but we want our faith to grow.

GROWTH:

God gives each believer a certain amount of faith (Romans 12:3). But like the muscles in our bodies, our faith can't grow stronger unless we exercise it. Two things that really give faith a workout are adversity and remembrance.

A trio in the Bible known as "the three Hebrew boys" modeled how adversity and remembrance will grow faith (Daniel chapters 1-3). We also see in their story how God rewards our faith.

In their adolescent years, these three (Shadrach, Meshach and Abednego) were stripped away from their parents, siblings, homes—everything they knew—and taken into captivity in a faraway land. Life there was nothing like what they were used to. Their captors spoke a different language, worshipped different gods, ate different foods, and lived different lives. Worst of all, these youngsters had no idea what had become of the loved ones they'd left behind. Were they crying out and grieving over the children they'd lost? Had they been taken somewhere and sold into slavery? Were they even alive, or had the armies killed them all? How traumatizing do you think that was for these kids?

Yet, when told to eat the food their captors provided, these youngsters chose to take a stand and honor their faith by sticking to the dietary restrictions their Jewish religion prescribed. They could have been punished or maybe even killed for doing so.

But God rewarded them for stepping out on faith in the face of adversity. He gave them an unusual aptitude for understanding literature and wisdom (Daniel chapter 1).

About a year later, the faith of these boys was tested again. This time it was a combination of adversity and remembrance that strengthened their faith.

The king had a dream that worried him, but he couldn't remember what it was. He threw a fit when nobody was able to tell him what the dream was and what it meant. He sent out a decree to kill every last magician, astrologer, sorcerer, and wise man in his kingdom. That would have included the three Hebrew boys and Daniel, their companion in the faith.

Instead of complaining to God about being in yet another life-or-death situation, they chose to remember who their great God was. They earnestly prayed for God to reveal the dream and its interpretation to Daniel. And God did just that.

Daniel told the king what his dream was and gave him the interpretation. Then the king withdrew his command to kill all the wise men, and he promoted Daniel, Shadrach, Meshach, and Abednego (Daniel chapter 2).

Now fast forward roughly nineteen years. That's when Shadrach, Meshach, and Abednego faced their biggest test of faith—the fiery furnace. In Daniel chapter 3, the king built a huge statue of himself and commanded that everyone bow down and worship it. But the three Hebrew boys let him know they would only worship the one true and living God.

Again, this madman threatened to kill them—this time by throwing them in a fiery furnace.

Shadrach, Meshach, and Abednego could have become discouraged and said to God, "Why do you keep letting one thing after another threaten our very lives? Why don't you make it stop? Haven't we been faithful to you? You obviously don't care for us anymore, so why should we care for you?"

But they would not allow their situation to dictate how they felt about God. They chose to remember who their God was and how great He was.

The king had upped the ante when he said to them,

> *"But if you refuse, you will be thrown immediately into the blazing furnace. And then what god will be able to rescue you from my power?"* (Daniel 3:15 NLT)

Well, the Hebrew boys didn't run to God and tell Him how big their problem was. They told their problem how big their God was when they said to the king,

> *"If we are thrown into the blazing furnace, the God whom we serve is able to save us. He will rescue us from your power, Your Majesty. But even if He doesn't, we want to make it clear to you, Your Majesty, that we will never serve your gods or worship the gold statue you have set up"* (Daniel 3:17-18 NLT).

Obviously, a *good* outcome would have been God intervening to stop the king from throwing them in the fire. To some of us, it would have been an even *better* outcome if God gave the king a taste of his own medicine by tossing him into the fire. But from God's perspective, the *greatest* outcome would occur by allowing his servants to face the fiery trial.

How could that be?

Well, the heat from the fiery furnace was so hot that it burned up the soldiers who were outside the incinerator shoving the Hebrew boys into it. What greater testament to God's power could there be than delivering His faithful servants out of that blazing inferno unharmed?

And that's just what God did.

Everyone was astounded when the Hebrew boys came out of that fire. Not only were they alive, but

---

... the fire had not touched them. Not a hair on their heads was singed, and their clothing was not scorched. They didn't even smell of smoke! (Daniel 3:27 NLT)

See the pattern here? Like us, each of the three Hebrew boys started out with a seed of faith. But each time adversity popped up in their lives, relying on God to get them through was what made their faith grow. Every one of their challenges was bigger than the one before it. Likewise, God's deliverance and reward was progressively greater each time.

The next time you go through something you wish you didn't have to face, ask God for guidance and strength, then flex those faith muscles.

The Bully

LIFE EXPERIENCE:

I recall learning to curse in the fourth grade at McCosh Elementary School in Chicago. I was actually a good kid, not one to use foul language. Up until fourth grade, my roughest words were "dag" and "heckie yeah." During the sixties in Chicago, "dag" was a non-curser's way of saying damn, and "heckie" was a replacement for the word hell. But my mom didn't even allow me to use those two pseudo curse words because she knew the meaning behind them.

Nevertheless, I spit out "dag" and "heckie yeah" around my friends at school every chance I got—to fit in I guess. (Don't tell my mom. I'm sixty and she still doesn't know this. And when I give her an autographed copy of this book, I'll *accidentally* tear out this chapter.)

In the fourth grade, I started to believe that using more offensive profanity was key to my survival. More bullies appeared in the fourth grade than there had been in the previous three grades. Sometimes there would be brawls, but I began to notice that more often than not, a fight was averted if someone threw around the real harsh four-letter words. Anytime someone tried to push you around, you just set 'em straight with a long flow of the roughest "cuss" words you could muster, and they would run off with their tail between their legs.

Or so I thought.

GROWTH:

My safety net was to talk the talk of the bullies so they wouldn't bully me. Without realizing it, we Christians sometimes speak the language of our enemy the devil, hoping it will make him stop bullying us. And he has a whole arsenal of weapons to bully us with: fear, rejection, doubt, division, jealousy, frustration, sadness, guilt, and many more.

He plants a seed in our minds. Maybe he says we're not loveable. Or we're a screw-up. Or we're not pretty enough, not slim enough. And what do we do? We assume it's the truth. Then, we speak it out of our own mouths. We crack jokes about ourselves ("You wouldn't believe what I did. I'm so stupid.") or put ourselves down ("I eat like a hog.") because we want to say it before someone else does. We don't even know if they think that way about us. But because we assume they do, we try to insulate our fragile self-esteem and take the sting out of the remark by beating them to the punch.

We give the enemy too much power over us when we believe and repeat what he says about us. The way to conquer this bully is to internalize and speak what God says about us.

When the enemy says you're unlovable, tell him that God says,

"The LORD has appeared of old to me, saying: "Yes, I have loved you with an everlasting love; Therefore with lovingkindness I have drawn you" (Jeremiah 31:3 NKJV).

"Because you are precious in My sight, you are honored and I love you..." (Isaiah 43:4 AMP).

When the enemy tries to put a chokehold on you because of your past, tell him that God says,

"Therefore, if anyone is in Christ, he is a new creation; old things have passed away; behold, all things have become new" (2 Corinthians 5:17 NKJV).

"There is therefore now no condemnation to those who are in Christ Jesus, who do not walk according to the flesh, but according to the Spirit" (Romans 8:1 NKJV).

"For all have sinned and fall short of the glory of God, being justified freely by His grace through the redemption that is in Christ Jesus" (Romans 3:23-24 NKJV).

When the enemy says you're weak, tell him that God says,

"... Let the weak say, 'I am strong'" (Joel 3:10 NKJV).

"I can do all things through Christ who strengthens me" (Philippians 4:13 NKJV).

Don't let that bully define you. As pastor and author Sunday Adelaja once said, "Your self-reliance, self-appraisal, and self-perception depends on how successful you are at knowing who God has created you to become."

What are you Expecting?

LIFE EXPERIENCE:

"I'm so sorry, but the procedure wasn't successful. You're not pregnant."

Five cycles of fertility treatments, and each one ended with the same sad news. I was devastated. All my life I'd wanted a child, but never thought of the possibility that it wouldn't happen. I loved children and couldn't understand why God would put such a strong desire in me, only to let it go unfulfilled. Whenever a news story came on about someone torturing or killing their innocent child "because they wouldn't stop crying" or "because the devil told me to do it," I was even more crushed. I asked God again and again why that person was allowed to have children, but I couldn't.

I'd come close twice. In my late thirties, I had a miscarriage before reaching the third month of my first pregnancy. Several years later, a tubal pregnancy caused the loss of my right fallopian tube. These two occurrences prompted me to eventually seek out a fertility specialist. So there I sat with my heart shattered because this was the last fertility treatment my insurance would pay for, and it hadn't worked.

Well-meaning friends asked if I'd thought about adoption. But that wasn't an option in my mind because more than anything, I longed to look at a child and see my face.

I couldn't escape my new reality. I was never going to bear a child.

Unless you have been in this position, you can't fully understand the amount of grieving that comes with it. Someone on the outside looking in might think, "How can you grieve over something you never had? I understand you feeling that way when you miscarried, and I would have understood if you had suffered a stillbirth or the loss of an actual child."

But for me and other infertile women, you grieve the loss of a dream. Sure, a child was something you hoped for, not a reality. But your hope and expectancy were so strong that the manifestation of it felt inevitable. And when you learn that it isn't, that dream you've nurtured dies.

So you mourn. You grieve. And you go through all the stages that a person grieving the loss of "an actual child" goes through. Denial. Anger. Bargaining. Depression. Acceptance.

It took a good two years for me to be at peace with my reality. Now I have to admit, I had my moments. Like when my cousin gave birth to her only son. She and I were raised to be like sisters, so naturally she called me from her hospital room after he was born. I heard him wailing in the background because the nurse had pricked his heel to test his blood sugar. A smile spread across my face as my cousin described what her newborn son looked like. I was genuinely happy for her. Yet I cried uncontrollably when I hung up the phone because I would never experience the elation she was feeling.

Thankfully, God had a means to soothe my hurt and compensate me for what I had lost. And it was definitely unexpected to me.

GROWTH:

I had known for a while that I was blessed with a gift for teaching God's Word. Previously, I had been called upon to teach in women's ministries and adult Bible studies. I even taught a class at an accredited Bible college in 2002. Then I was asked to teach in the children's ministry at the church I attended in 2007.

You might think that was an answer to my prayer.

But I was terrified. I knew how to connect with the adults I taught. I could explain things in a way they could relate to. But I was not around children often. What if the little ones at church couldn't relate to me? What if I couldn't reach them? I didn't have any children. How was I supposed to know how to speak their language? I didn't know what kinds of things they liked. I wasn't sure I could communicate in a way that they'd understand.

Aside from all that, what if they just flat out didn't like me?

Despite my concerns, I took the assignment. And wouldn't you know it? It was just what I needed. The children were drawn to me, and I certainly loved working with them. I treasured the unexpected things they'd say. Like when I was playing Hokey Pokey with a group of preschoolers, one little boy took my hand, dragged me to the middle of the circle of dancing kids, looked me in the eyes and serenaded me. "You put your *old* self in. You take your *old* self out. You put your *old* self in and you shake it all about." You can correct me if I'm wrong, but I'm pretty sure the song says, "You put your *whole* self in."

I had lots of laughs while teaching the children. I probably learned just as much from them as they learned from me. And most of all, I got to experience the joy of having a group of children run up to me, screaming my name ("Ms. Janice, Ms. Janice") and offering hugs and high fives.

The words of Isaiah 61:3 come to mind, where God promises to give us a spirit of praise in place of a spirit of sadness. God knew the mothering instinct He put inside me would make me successful in that teaching assignment. That's why He gave me that avenue to tap into and satisfy that need.

He did an even more marvelous thing when He blessed me to marry Pastor Sammie Allen, Sr. in 2019. Pastor Allen was a widower with four grown children, four grandchildren, and a great grandchild on the way. When his beloved wife passed away after forty-plus years of marriage, he had no desire to ever wed again. As for me, I was two years post-divorce in 2019. After nineteen years in that marriage, I too had the "never again" mindset. Pastor and I attest to the fact that only God could have put us together. Neither of us saw it coming, but we were truly pleased when God revealed His plan for us.

God gave me an unexpected gift when He put me in the Allen family. Finding your place in a blended family isn't always the easiest thing. But over time, God did a work on my heart and on the children's hearts. He eased our reservations and opened our eyes so that we could see and appreciate each other for who we really were. The bond between me, the children, the grandchildren, and the great grandchild, continues to grow. I'll never try to replace their mother/grandmother. That would be impossible to do, and that's not why God placed me here. But I am thankful for the opportunity to be a nurturing presence and a trusted friend in their lives.

Philippians 1:6 says,

God began doing a good work in you, and I am sure he will continue it until it is finished when Jesus Christ comes again (NCV).

Long story short—if God places something in you, you can be certain that He will open a door for you to use it to glorify Him. And how He chooses to accomplish that might be in a way you least expect.

Move Out of the Way

LIFE EXPERIENCE:

Lazy bums. That's the only way to describe me and my friend Angela that summer day—me lounging on her creaky wooden porch swing and her sitting on a wicker chair reading to Ryan, a three-year-old replica of her husband Josh.

A shiny, new lawnmower sat in the middle of the asphalt driveway. Grooming their enormous yard was one of Josh's passions. Bounding up the porch stairs two at a time, Josh came and grabbed the thermos perched on the top step. He took a long swig of ice water, then playfully swatted at his son before heading back to the yard.

Ryan became fussy. He scooted off his mom's lap and tugged on her hand until she got up and allowed him to lead her into the house. While they were inside, Josh made two superfast passes across the lawn with his mower. He'd be done in no time at this pace.

Angela came back outside carrying a toy lawnmower in her hand and her son on her hip. Ryan's eyes were filled with excitement as she placed him and his bubble mower near the swatch of grass Josh had already mowed. The little tyke obviously had his mind set on helping his dad. Mighty Mouse to the rescue.

Leaving his mower idling, Josh walked to Ryan and bent down to pour bubble solution in the plastic lawnmower. He gave his apprentice a few words of instruction, and off they both went, mowing the yard.

Josh had to slow down to a snail's pace to accommodate his son's small steps.

The junior lawn man crept behind his dad, pushing the bubble mower over grass that his father's mower had just cut. He kept looking behind and grinning at us, pleased at the results of *his* labor and oblivious to the fact that it wasn't his mower that was getting the job done.

Less than three minutes later, Ryan abandoned his mower. He came to sit on the bottom step of the porch and Angela handed him half a Popsicle. The youngster chewed on the treat, dripping it onto his shirt, his pants, and the ground. My eyes were glued to a line of ants moving across the sidewalk to join the party.

While Ryan took his break, Josh put the pedal to the metal. He whipped the lawnmower up and down that yard so fast that I feared he might pass out from heat stroke. And just as he got into a flow, his trainee, now full of sugar, walked back to his bubble mower, ready to punch the clock again.

Josh's speed dropped to almost zero to accommodate the tiny warrior who fell in line behind him.

All told, Josh spent twice as long getting the job done—because his son wanted to help.

GROWTH:

Little Ryan's good intentions backfired, causing it to take a much longer time for his father's plan to come to fruition. This got me thinking. How many times have I caused God's plan for my life to be delayed because I got in His way while trying to help Him? And unlike Ryan, I have even run out in front of my Father, not waiting for Him to clear a path for me, but trying to do it on my own. Instead of waiting to hear His plan and following His lead, I would tell Him my plan—then expect Him to be content to follow behind me. When things fell apart— as they often did under these circumstances—I'd pout and go sit on the sidelines, only to be amazed to see God step in and effortlessly do the thing I was struggling to accomplish.

There are numerous instances of the Bible telling us to wait on the Lord.

Wait on the Lord; be of good courage, and He shall strengthen your heart; wait, I say, on the Lord! (Psalm 27:14 NKJV)

... But those who wait on the Lord, they shall inherit the earth (Psalm 37:9 NKJV).

My soul, wait silently for God alone, for my expectation is from Him (Psalm 62:5 NKJV).

The Lord is good to those who wait for Him, to the soul who seeks Him (Lamentations 3:25 NKJV).

But waiting can be such a challenge. We feel like we have to be doing something to move toward our goal. And that's fine because waiting doesn't mean you have to be idle. For example, while you're waiting for God to bless you with that new house, how about doing things to prepare yourself for that blessing? Make it a habit to thank God for your current living space and for the new place you desire. Become more appreciative of what you already have and take the best care of it that you can. Make time to get rid of anything you wouldn't take into your wonderful new abode. Get your credit straight so you can get a better interest rate.

Perhaps we all need to think again the next time we are tempted to pull out our little bubble mowers and help God mow down the problems in our life. Sometimes He wants us to stay on the porch while He does all the heavy lifting.

Rest for Your Soul

LIFE EXPERIENCE:

Have you ever tried to snooze with a sleeping toddler next to you? The baby takes over the bed. She might start out snuggling under you, but before you know it, she is spread eagle in the middle of the bed, then diagonal with her feet under your armpits, finally ending up with her head on your ankle as she softly snores through tiny nostrils.

In spite of all her movement, she rests peacefully. Meanwhile, your sleep, if you get any at all, is broken and shallow. No matter how exhausted you are, you can't fully doze off because you don't know where the child will move to next. You don't want to roll over on her or accidentally push her out of the bed. So all night, you sleep with one eye open, repositioning yourself around this rough-sleeping critter as she slumbers soundly.

This child, who has so completely given in to her body's need to rest, without a word commands you to move out of her way all night long.

GROWTH:

Now let's re-imagine that scene. See the child as symbolizing you. The bed represents your life, and the adult represents the obstacles and mountains that have "climbed into bed" with you, so to speak. How many sleepless nights have the problems in your life caused? Your body is drained but your brain won't shut down because you can't stop the thoughts running through your head. *How will I get the money to pay the rent before we get put out on the street? Where will I get enough food to feed my family one more day? Can everyone I love survive this COVID-19 crisis? How did my child get on drugs? How could I not see it until it was too late?*

Nobody escapes trouble; not those who believe in God, not those who don't. But it's a real victory when we can find rest for our souls in the midst of the trials and tribulations that are sure to come our way. David gave us a great example at a time when his life was being turned upside down. He was on the run because his own son had conspired to kill him and take his crown. In his distress, David said,

---

Lord, I have many enemies! Many people have turned against me. Many are saying about me, "God won't rescue him." Selah. But, Lord, you are my shield, my wonderful God who gives me courage. I will pray to the Lord, and he will answer me from his holy mountain. Selah. I can lie down and go to sleep, and I will wake up again, because the Lord gives me strength (Psalm 3:1-5 NCV).

David's troubles were very real, but in spite of them, he found solace because he cried out to the Lord and God heard him. Being assured of God's presence gave David so much peace that he could lay down, rest, and awake refreshed, for his mind and spirit had been calmed.

God demonstrated this to me several years ago when I had to take someone to court. Just like the big bad wolf, my opponent was huffing, and puffing, and threatening to blow my house down. After a while, it wore on me. I was distraught with worry. Every second of the day, my mind mulled over the situation. One sleepless night followed the next.

Then God reassured me through a dream.

In this dream, I was a toddler in a huge room. Aside from me, nothing else occupied the space except for a huge vacuum cleaner. It stood in the middle of the floor and was pointed in my direction. Mind you, it wasn't moving, but it was turned on, making a terrifying noise, and kicking up lots of dust.

The thought of it crossing that room and eating me alive petrified me. It was so big and powerful. I was so small and helpless.

Suddenly, I sensed the presence of my Heavenly Father, and boy was I glad. I just knew He was going to crush the thing that threatened to take me out.

He didn't do that.

My next thought was that He'd at least unplug the contraption so the horrifying noise would cease.

He didn't do that either.

"He's going to speak up and command the thing to stop, or leave, or both," I reasoned.

I was right. He did speak—but not to the vacuum cleaner. Instead, He quietly spoke to me, His child.

"I'm with you, and I need you to know that. I am your protection. I need you to believe that. I will keep you safe until I declare that the threat is over. I will get you through this, so I need you to focus on My presence more than on the problem."

The vacuum cleaner revved its motor. The sound was deafening and the room became dark from the cloud of black smoke and dust spewing from it. Yet, I was enveloped in peace.

In a matter of minutes, God prompted me to leave the room. Interestingly enough, He didn't have me creep along the wall to stay out of the machine's reach. He led me right through the middle of the room. I walked within centimeters of the vacuum, which was still making its vicious threats. But I wasn't afraid. With a calm spirit, I left the room.

From that time on, I was unafraid as I pursued and eventually won my court case.

My prayer is that just as the toddler in the beginning of this chapter yielded to her rest, you will surrender to the rest that God offers. Then the obstacles and mountains in your life will have no choice but to get out of your way as you peacefully move about the bed of life.

Stretch Out

LIFE EXPERIENCE:

Writing books is not something I aspired to do. As a child, I wanted to do one of two things when I grew up. Being a nurse appealed to me because I was fascinated by a television show called *Julia*. The idea of being a schoolteacher fascinated me too, but only because of how much I loved to write on chalkboards.

I pursued neither. My career choices included six years as a radio personality in Little Rock, Arkansas, a year as a flight attendant for the now defunct Pan Am Airlines, and thirty years as a legal secretary in Chicago.

So how did I start writing? At one of the law firms where I worked, I met a fellow legal secretary who had written and published several novels. I had always been an avid reader, but I'd never met a real live author, so I was captivated as we talked about her writing. Days later, I purchased several of her books, read them, and offered some constructive criticism. She was so impressed at the things I pointed out that she said I had the makings of a good editor. After I immersed myself in some resources she recommended, she took me under her wing and taught me to edit her manuscripts.

My hidden writing ability became apparent to her through the work I was doing for her. She declared one day, "You don't know it, but you're a great writer." From there, she invited me to join a group of authors who were putting together a manual about writing, editing, and publishing.

Although my ability to write had been uncovered, I declined because letting my creativity flow through the pen was a grueling task. Being analytical and detail-oriented helped me to be a good editor, but those qualities proved to be a double-edged sword because they neutralized my creative element when it came to composing. Before settling on the perfect words to put on the page, I'd write and re-write something a million times in my head.

In spite of all that, I finally gathered the nerve to co-author that self-help manual for aspiring writers in 2014 called *Baring it All: The Ins and Outs of Publishing*. Several years later, I wrote and published two novels and a short story, then authored and published this Christian inspirational book. Don't get me wrong. I still dislike the process of writing a book because it remains a hard task for me. However, each time I reach the finish line, I am thoroughly pleased with the end result.

GROWTH:

Difficult and impossible are not one and the same. If something is impossible, it cannot be done at all. But a difficult task, no matter how demanding it may be, is within your power to accomplish. We all have some difficult undertakings. What if we looked at these things from a different perspective?

Did you ever shoot rubber bands at others when you were a child? You'd hook it on the tip of your thumb, use your other hand to draw the rubber band back, take aim, and let it fly. Next thing you knew, you were being chased by the unlucky target who felt the sting of your elastic weapon.

I wasn't good at this. The rubber bands I tried to shoot usually ended up flying just a few inches before dropping to the ground. Sometimes they even backfired, with me popping my own trigger finger. At a family reunion, I was laughing about this with my cousin, Pastor Steve Walker. He said that just like a bow and arrow, the secret to making the rubber band fly farther was to stretch it as far as you could.

God sometimes allows circumstances to stretch us almost to our breaking point. But it's never meant to make us snap. The purpose is to propel us farther into our destiny. Queen Esther in the Bible is a great example.

Orphaned when she was young, Esther was taken in by Mordecai, an older cousin. He loved her as if she were his own child. She was a beautiful and obedient girl.

The Persian king was searching for a new queen, and he planned to choose from among the young virgins in the land. Esther was included in that number. Like the other females, she had no choice in the matter. Because she and Mordecai were Jewish exiles living in the Persian empire, he instructed her to conceal her heritage.

The king loved Esther above all the others, and chose her to be his queen.

You might think that she had it made in the shade. She went from refugee to ruler. But God was going to use this new position to stretch Esther.

One day Haman, one of the king's noblemen, became enraged when Mordecai refused to bow to him. It wasn't enough for him to seek to kill Mordecai. Haman, who was anti-Semitic, tricked the king into signing an edict stating that on a specified day, the Persian people would be allowed to attack and kill all Jewish people.

Mordecai sent word to Esther about what was happening, adding that she needed to appeal to the king on behalf of her people. The gravity of the situation didn't escape her. But she had a dilemma. Approaching the king to bring up the situation would put her in jeopardy because no one, not even the queen, was granted an audience before the king unless he called for them. Those who dared to do otherwise were put to death.

Her cousin reminded her that if Haman's planned genocide took place, being in the king's house would not provide her with a safety net. Her true heritage would be discovered and she would be killed along with all the other Jews.

Esther now understood that being elevated to the position of queen had been more than a stroke of luck to benefit her alone. God had placed her in a position where she might influence the outcome of her people. Her initial response of "I might be killed if I go and speak to the king" turned into "I will go to the king, and if he kills me, he kills me."

After fasting for three days, she presented herself before the king, and he welcomed her. She invited the king and Haman to join her for banquets on two nights. The night of the second banquet, she pleaded with the king to save her life and the lives of her people. When the king asked who sought their lives, she revealed Haman's plan and the fact that she was a Jewess. She could have been killed for having deceived the king. However, the king loved her so much that he had Haman and his sons hanged because of Haman's conniving and treachery.

But a problem still existed. The king could not rescind an order he'd given. So the decree that Persians could kill any and all Jews on a set date still stood. Esther petitioned the king, and the Jews were granted permission to defend themselves against those who sought to slaughter them. Instead of being wiped out, the Jewish people killed over 75,000 of their enemies.

Esther had a quiet and submissive nature. But she allowed herself to be stretched into becoming an advocate for her people. Her actions prevented the annihilation of the entire Jewish population in Persia.

How is God using your challenges to stretch you? He worked through my struggles with writing to stretch me. Many aspiring authors told me they were helped by what I shared in Baring It All. Opening up about the difficulties I faced let them know they were not the only ones going through it, and encouraged them to press forward in their writing careers. Others have told me they were blessed by the moral and spiritual lessons they gleaned from this book and my novels.

Maybe you won't save a nation like Esther did, but your calling might be to save a teen who's teetering on the edge. Or a mother who's about to throw up her hands and walk away from her child. Or a co-worker who's ready to go postal. God has placed certain people in your path who you are to bless, mentor, and even save from destruction. They are the targets before you. But you'll never penetrate the target unless you allow yourself to be stretched and propelled into your destiny.

Knowing His Voice

LIFE EXPERIENCE:

My goddaughter Raven is now an adult with a toddler of her own. But I remember being astounded by something Raven did when she was a newborn.

My mom and I were sitting at the dinner table visiting with Raven and her parents. We cooed and marveled at Raven as she worked hard to polish off her four-ounce bottle of formula. Her mom then placed her on her shoulder and patted her back to burp her. Everything went as planned ... that is, until Raven's dad spoke.

Upon hearing her father's voice, Raven launched her head in his direction, catapulting her head and torso from the left side of her mom's chest and shoulder to the right side. Had her mother not instinctively held on tighter, the infant could have flung herself to the floor. I nearly had a heart attack, but Raven's mom was calm.

She said, "That happens all the time. Her dad used to talk to her through my stomach when I was pregnant with her. And now whenever she hears his voice, she leans his way. The first time it happened, she moved so hard and fast that she almost jumped out of my arms. Now I'm ready for it."

GROWTH:

John 10:27 says

My sheep hear my voice, and I know them, and they follow me (KJV).

Unimaginable things happen when a believer wholeheartedly throws him or herself into hearing God's voice. That tiny baby's entire body gravitated toward the sound of her father's voice. Christians should be equally perceptive of, and responsive to, the voice of God.

Sometimes God puts other people in our lives to prepare us to hear from Him. Rev. Renee Sesvalah Cobb-Dishman was one of those people. One year, we shared a hotel room when we attended an author's event. Before we left the room that Saturday morning, she told me God had given her a word of prophecy for me, and asked if it would be okay for her to share it with me. I said all right and sat down.

"God says that no matter what it looks like, He's got your back," she stated.

"I receive it," I replied without hesitation. I was in the midst of a difficult divorce that was filled with one delaying and disappointing court date after another. And each time my lawyer appeared before the judge on my behalf, it seemed as if he returned with bad news. So hearing this reminder that God had my back was just the encouragement and assurance I needed then.

She continued. "God is sending a man who wants to be kind to you and to be a companion. All he wants to do is love you."

Honestly, I shut down upon hearing those words. Loving someone, or being loved by someone, was the furthest thing from my mind. As stated in the "What Are You Expecting?" chapter of this book, my mind was made up that I'd never do the marriage thing again. In fact, I had already resolved that after the divorce was finalized and I became a single woman, I would never so much as date again. Dating leads to feelings. Feelings lead to relationships. Relationships lead to marriage. And I was never going to put myself through that kind of ordeal again.

My friend placed a hand on my shoulder and said, "Don't block God's blessings and don't box Him in. Be open to His blessings manifesting in unexpected ways."

That softened my heart. Not to the idea of dating, relationships, or marriage, mind you, but to the importance of being open to God. And I'm so glad God spoke to me through her. Otherwise, I would have blocked the blessing that manifested in my life three years later—my husband, Pastor Sammie Allen, Sr.

He and I jokingly say that ours is a marriage made in heaven because only God could have brought us together the way He did. Any number of thoughts and obstacles could have kept us apart. For instance, some family members and friends were skeptical about our short and secretive courtship. The fact that one of us was going to have to uproot our entire life and relocate across the country—leaving behind loved ones, churches, vocations, etc.—could have been a deterrent as well. Additionally, before God brought us together, we had both decided that love for our families and the joy we found in our ministry work would fulfill us and supersede the need or desire for another mate. That resolve could have caused us to make different decisions about having a future together. But when God spoke to Pastor and told Him I would be his wife, he willingly obeyed. His only request was that God would enlarge his heart because he had truly loved his late wife and did not want in any way to let that shortchange the love he could have for the new wife God had for him. During that same time, God was also preparing my heart for marriage.

The day came when Pastor shared with me over the phone what God had spoken to Him.

Pastor: "Are you sitting down or standing up?"

Me: "I'm lying down. It's 9:45 there in California, but it's almost midnight here in Illinois."

Pastor: "Well, I have something to tell you. God says you're going to be my wife."

Me: A slight pause, followed by, "Okay."

Though surprised to get a positive response without the skepticism a declaration like his could have evoked, he was definitely relieved. Our never-ending phone conversations over the prior months had cultivated in me a deep respect for, and an attraction to, the man that Sammie is. I shared this with him after he told me what God said about me being his wife. We laughed when I added that had God not orchestrated this, we would have lived the rest of our lives being good friends on the phone and I would have gone to my grave without ever letting him know I had developed feelings for him.

Getting married was a leap of faith for both of us, and I love living life with my Sammie. Though we had obstacles to overcome, we'd be the first to tell you there is great reward when you listen to and obey God's voice. Our experience with God bringing us together is living proof that God means just what He says in Proverbs 3:5-6.

> *Trust in the Lord with all your heart, and lean not on your own understanding; in all your ways acknowledge Him, and He shall direct your paths* (NKJV).

A final scripture that comes to mind is Psalm 37:4.

> *Delight yourself also in the Lord: and He shall give you the desires of your heart* (NKJV).

Many people interpret this to mean that God will give you whatever you desire if you delight in Him. But Sammie and I have come to know that the greater meaning is that when you delight to align yourself with the will of God, He will show your heart what it should desire. And believe me, what God wants for you is far better than anything you could want for yourself.

Release It

LIFE EXPERIENCE:

A few years back, I attended a rather unique women's prayer breakfast. The speaker shared with us some of the pains she had suffered in life. The death of both parents within six months of each other. Grieving a beloved grandmother who no longer knew her granddaughter due to dementia. Losing her son because her ex-husband's wealth gave him an advantage in their custody battle. Then the gut-punch of finding out she had breast cancer.

These back-to-back catastrophes had brought her to her knees. Suicide had even crossed her mind a time or two. But her story of suffering turned into a testimony of redemption. She shared how God showed her that she could not get past any of this until she let go of the bitterness and pain, and sought His healing.

One table in the room had a centerpiece made up of a colorful bouquet of helium balloons on strings. She invited each of us to choose a balloon then told us to use the magic markers at our tables to write on our balloon the things we needed to let go of.

While we wrote, the speaker stood at the microphone and quietly prayed a scripture.

"Then Jesus said, 'Come to me, all of you who are weary and carry heavy burdens, and I will give you rest. Take my yoke upon you. Let me teach you, because I am humble and gentle at heart, and you will find rest for your souls. For my yoke is easy to bear, and the burden I give you is light'" (Matthew 11:28-30 NLT).

She continued to repeat that to us. With each recitation, the floodgate of emotions in the room opened a little more. The more we wrote, the more we wept.

The balloons now wore our sorrows.

After a few minutes, we were able to regain our composure—for the most part. We had wiped away our tears, but the heaviness was still present and tangible.

The speaker asked us to get our balloons and follow her outside. She led us in prayer, thanking God for release and restoration. More tears flowed. Then she told us to open our eyes and let go of our balloons.

GROWTH:

As you might have guessed, this symbolized releasing our bitterness and pain. But when I first let my balloon go, something made me reach up and grab the string to pull it back down before it got out of reach. Why? I didn't suddenly think of something else I needed to write on it. Just instinct, I guess. After all, that was my stuff, my sadness, my pain.

Through that action, I could clearly see that sometimes the issue wasn't that my pain wouldn't leave me. The reality had often been that I refused to let go of the pain.

What a revelation that was.

Once again, I let go of the string, this time allowing the balloon to drift away. It only took a second for it to be just out of reach but still within view. Then it was higher than the steeple of the church we stood beside. Before I could take five or six more breaths, it was just a red dot on the clouds. In another blink, it disappeared from view.

Psalm 147:3 says,

He heals the brokenhearted and binds up their wounds (NKJV).

I am grateful for the lesson I learned that day. This unforgettable visual representation from God will always be a reminder that if I am willing to let go of past pain, He will strip it of its power to harm, and turn it into an instrument of healing.

Epilogue

As I close, I want to share an entry from my journal. I went through Christian counseling in my early fifties because I was tired of how I was allowing myself to be mistreated. It wasn't hard to connect the dots and see how childhood sexual abuse had laid the groundwork for my victim mentality in adulthood. But I didn't have the slightest clue how to create a different Janice, one who would value herself enough to not accept abuse, especially emotional abuse.

You're probably saying, "You could have just left the abusive person." And you're right; that was an option. However, until I understood what it was inside of me that allowed me to keep putting myself in the hands of people who would abuse me, I'd be helpless to break the cycle. I would inevitably leave one abuser, only to end up in a new abusive relationship. That's why getting help from a Christian counselor was essential to my healing.

"Gift from God" is one of the meanings of the name Janice. Yet, I had spent the better part of my life not seeing myself as a gift, but more like a last-place prize. I'm grateful to God that over the course of counseling, I came to embrace the fact that He created me in His image. How special is that?

The below entry from my journal was written to the man who abused me during my childhood. Though he died many years before I wrote it, I learned in counseling that my healing didn't depend on him reading it; it depended on me being able to connect with the negative feelings I had bottled up inside and tap into a strength I didn't know was there. So it was June of 2014 when I found my voice and my strength. I pray that these words, as well as the others in this book, will encourage you and give you the resolve to grow.

June 12, 2014

I'm glad you are no longer here because I can hate you without feeling guilty about whether or not my hatred might hurt you. I know it's said that God hates the sin, not the sinner. Well, I hate you (the sinner) more than I hate what you did to me (the sin).

What woman were you thinking of when you had this scrawny little girl laid on her back? Was I a convenient living blow-up doll to play your fantasies out on? Because I didn't know how to say no, didn't even know I had a right to say no, did you take that to mean that I desired you?

If you were still alive, I wonder if you would find shame in the fact that you—a grown man with all the emotional, mental, and financial resources to reach out for someone to help you through whatever issues you were struggling with—turned to a helpless child and laid all your filth, issues, and debauchery at her feet.

Let me say it again so you can hear it, because you obviously never let yourself grasp this truth—I WAS A CHILD! Because of what you did, I was a child who never learned to live in the moment. In those humiliating incidences of molestation, I automatically shut down emotionally. It was an internal mechanism to protect my unformed psyche against the shock, guilt, and shame of what you were doing to me. But the same defense mechanism that provided a shield during the episodes of childhood sexual abuse would prove to be a noose that strangled my emotional development. It caused me to walk through my adulthood always on guard and ready to shut my emotions down. So I have moved from one day to the next without being able to fully experience life.

But I finally got the memo that I am letting my life slide by. Now I want to engage with my life. I want to laugh so hard that I feel it in my toes. I want to cry until my stomach turns inside out. I want to finish every day knowing that I loved, laughed, cried, and experienced my time on earth.

I don't want to keep being bound by that ghost inside of me that says I need to fade into the background. You know, that phantom you planted there when your actions left me with the notion that I—a quiet, skinny, plain-Jane 11-year-old girl—caused you to molest me. I want to do more than tune out that voice. I want to hit the delete button so that it is permanently erased from existence. Never again do I want to feel like I should be invisible. I might not be the prettiest crayon in the box, but I intend to become the brightest neon-colored one that I can, and glow in spite of the darkness your cruelty shrouded me in. I want to be seen! I want to be treasured! I want to be cherished! Not only did you not give me this, but you cut off in my mind the possibility of me ever getting it, of ever deserving it. In the past, I used to wish you would have told me why you did this to me. But now it doesn't matter. I think if you ever had found the guts to tell me, you would have just twisted it somehow to take the ugliness out of it.

So I'll remember this 2014 day as a new start for me. Too bad you didn't see me for the wonderful little person I was back then. Too bad you're not alive to see who I'm growing into. And honestly, I'm glad you're gone because that makes it somewhat easier for me to forgive you. If you were here, I would choose to haul around my unforgiveness and all the baggage that goes with it, instead of forgiving you. If you were alive, forgiving you would feel like giving you a pat on the hand and saying what you did was excusable or understandable. But because you're not here, I can forgive you. I can endeavor to release myself from all the bad things that came out of what you did to me. I can do that and have the satisfaction of knowing I'm not giving you a pass on what you did.

I've got a bucket list in my mind. Nothing extra adventurous, just things I want to do that will make me feel like I'm living out all of my potential. I want to learn to read music so I can play the piano much better than I do now. I want to learn to draw and paint. I actually don't have any drawing or art skills, but I admire people who have the ability to see something and recreate it on paper or canvas, so I'd like to tap into that experience just for the fun of it. I want to take martial arts, for the physical conditioning as well as the mental focus. Little by little, I'm putting my ducks in a row so I can free up time to develop me and my desires. This is me taking back my life. This is me pouring fluorescent paint over myself and walking through the darkness you sentenced me to exist in.

I'm coming out of the darkness!

THAT WAS WRITTEN IN 2014. From that day to this one, I can say with confidence, humility, and thanksgiving that God has refreshed and restored my soul. I pray that you experience the same through your relationship with God.

Janice M. Allen

National Bestselling author Janice M. Allen is living proof that it's never too late to grow and blossom. She uncovered her gift of writing in 2014 when she co-authored Baring It All: The Ins and Outs of Publishing, a self-help manual for writers.

Her foray into fiction began with her first novel, No Right Way to do a Wrong Thing, which was released in 2018 and became a two-time AALBC Bestseller. She followed that with the short story Cayenne.

Janice and eight other authors collaborated to co-write a romance novel called Kings of the Castle in November 2019. Janice's novel King of Lawndale is one of eight follow-up novels released in that series.

Growth is her first Christian inspirational book, and she is currently writing a second Christian inspirational book. Janice and her husband Pastor Sammie Allen, Sr. reside in Ridgecrest, California.

Website: www.janicemallen.com

Facebook Author Page:
https://www.facebook.com/JaniceAllen7519

Twitter: https://mobile.twitter.com/JaniceAllen7519

Instagram: https://www.instagram.com/janiceallen7519

Amazon Author Page:
Janice M. Allen's Amazon Author Page

Bookbub: Janice M. Allen on Bookbub

Sociatap: https://sociatap.com/janiceallen/

ALSO BY JANICE M. ALLEN

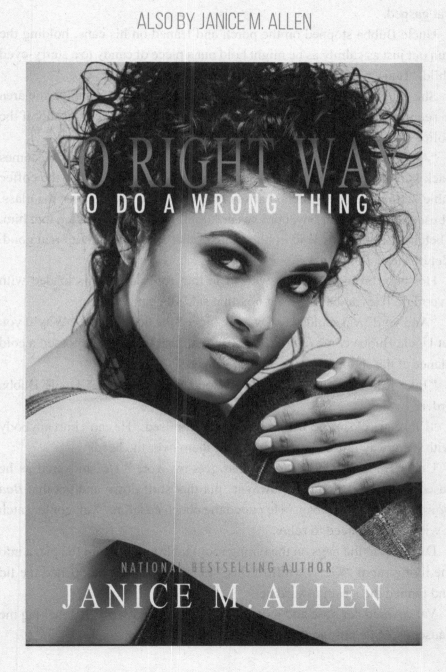

NO RIGHT WAY
TO DO A WRONG THING

NATIONAL BESTSELLING AUTHOR
JANICE M. ALLEN

EXCERPT FROM NO RIGHT WAY TO DO A WRONG THING

"I know you're not walking around in broad daylight with a shotgun," Val gasped.

Uncle Bubba stopped on the porch and leaned on his cane, holding the gun out just as calmly as he might hold out a piece of candy to a starry-eyed child. "It ain't real, Val."

She caught his arm and yanked him inside the house, scanning the area to see if any neighbors were nearby. "It's real enough to get you shot if the police see you with it."

"And it's real enough to keep that husband of yours in line if he comes back here actin' a fool," Uncle Bubba replied. He laid it across the coffee table, letting the heavy metal barrel clink a little too hard against the glass. "I used to respect that boy, but I swear I don't know what's gotten into him. I betcha if I put some lead in him though, that'll tighten him up real good. Get his head on straight."

Her twin brother Dwayne walked in the front door, arms loaded with overnight bags and a carry-out box that said Beggars Pizza.

"And you!" Val scolded as Dwayne kicked the door closed. "Why'd you let Uncle Bubba come out of the house with that thing?" She tossed a cold glance at the shotgun.

"Take it in the other room if you don't want to see it," Uncle Bubba ordered.

"I'll keep a close eye on him," Dwayne promised. "He can't hurt anybody with it anyway unless he uses it to beat them over the head."

Uncle Bubba nodded. "Yeah, that gets my vote." He snickered as he eased down on the couch. "Dwayne, put that stuff down and get that *Bad Boys* DVD out of my bag." He patted the couch cushion. "Val, come watch it with me. You need to relax."

Dwayne sat the bags on the dining room table and brought the pizza into the living room. "Get a whiff of this," he said to Val as he opened the lid and fanned the steam toward her.

Val covered her nose and jerked her head the other way. "It's making me nauseous." She pushed the box away.

"I'm sorry, li'l sis. I guess I have to get used to you being pregnant." He took the box in the dining room and came back with the movie.

"You're not too sick to sit with me, are ya?" Uncle Bubba asked Val as Dwayne loaded the DVD player.

She laid a hand on her stomach, trying to settle the queasiness. "No, Uncle Bubba. That, I can do."

"I'm going to have some pizza," Dwayne said as he headed toward the kitchen.

Uncle Bubba scooted over, and Val curled up beside him. Her head settled on his shoulder and she prayed that peace would tiptoe into her soul.

ᴨ ᴨ ᴨ

Val awoke two hours later to a room that was completely dark except for the brightness of the screen on the sixty-inch plasma tv. She lifted her head from Uncle Bubba's shoulder and fluffed her hair where it had gotten flat while she slept.

"Told you that you needed to rest," he said, patting her gently on the arm. "You didn't slobber on me, did you?" He inspected his sleeve.

She gave him a playful nudge with her shoulder, then pried herself off of the sofa and stretched. Headlights in the driveway and the unmistakable hum of her husband's SUV made her whole body tense up. Suddenly she found it hard to breathe.

Kurt. Dwayne. Uncle Bubba. The shotgun.

Nothing but trouble waiting to happen.

Uncle Bubba called for Dwayne. "Come down here, boy, and pass me my piece."

Dwayne's footsteps clattered overhead, followed by him rushing down the stairs. "I thought you said Kurt had to stay out of the house for forty-eight hours," he said to Val as he made it to the landing.

"That's what the police said."

Dwayne rounded the corner and went straight for the shotgun. Val went straight for the cordless phone in the kitchen.

"I'm calling the police," she said, scurrying back to the living room the moment Kurt's key slid in the first of the two locked doors.

Uncle Bubba grunted with the effort to get off of the couch. "Val, put the phone down," he said in a muffled tone. "We got this under control."

She shivered but relented, her hands shaking as she laid the phone on the love seat. "Uncle Bubba, that is just a toy gun, right?" she whispered back.

He didn't bother to answer.

Dwayne took up a position behind the door. Val stood frozen in place, praying that yellow crime scene tape wouldn't soon decorate her home.

The last lock clicked and Kurt tipped into the semi-dark house. "Now look, Val, I don't want any trouble," he said as he felt for the switch on the wall. "I just need to get my—"

Uncle Bubba cleared his throat as soon as the decorative ceiling light came on.

Kurt's gaze traveled from the old man to the shotgun he held at his side.

Dwayne stepped from behind the door.

Kurt glared at the two men like they were bullies on the playground. "Did you have to get involved in our business?"

Dwayne positioned himself protectively in front of Val. "My sister is my business." He gestured to the rest of the house. "The police having to come to this camp is our business."

Peeking around Dwayne's sturdy body, Val asked, "Why are you here?"

Kurt's gaze remained locked on Dwayne.

"You heard the girl," Uncle Bubba prodded. "What do you want?"

"I just needed to get a few things," Kurt said, his gaze darting around the room, probably trying to find some object to protect himself with.

"Well, me and Dwayne here are gonna do you like the cops prob'ly did you," Uncle Bubba advised. "We gonna escort you through the house so you can grab what you need and get to steppin'."

Dwayne took a few steps forward and reached for Kurt's elbow.

Kurt wrenched away. "Man, don't put your hands on me. This is my house," he said, clenching his teeth and thumping his chest with his index finger.

"You wait one cotton-pickin' minute," Uncle Bubba said, raising the stock of the shotgun to his shoulder and cocking the pump action.

All sound left the room.

Val's legs felt as though they were dissolving under her own weight. But she wouldn't give Kurt the satisfaction of seeing her blatant terror. She jutted her chin out and crossed her arms, matching Dwayne's stance.

A car door slammed outside. A few seconds later, the doorbell rang.

"Mama, I thought I told you to stay in the truck," Kurt answered without turning to face the door.

"She your bodyguard now?" Uncle Bubba taunted, the barrel still aimed at Kurt.

"Is everything all right, son?" Kurt's mother asked through the door. There was a slight, dull bump on the door as if she had pressed her head against it to listen in on what was happening inside.

"He'll be right out, Mama Melva," Val said loudly, motioning for Dwayne to hurry up and take Kurt to get his stuff so he could leave. A brisk burst of air swept over Val as the two men rushed past her. Uncle Bubba brought up the rear, his "phony" shotgun still trained on Kurt.

Mrs. Timmons' footsteps crossed the porch, clicked along the sidewalk, and then the SUV door opened and closed.

Three minutes later, Val's guardian angels were ushering Kurt to the front door. A laptop was in his left hand. With the other hand, he hung onto a pair of dress shoes with black socks stuffed in them. Two shirts and two pairs of slacks still on the hangers were draped over his right arm. The shaving kit, toothbrush and clean underwear sitting atop the pants and shirts were poised to slide to the floor. He jostled his belongings, trying to open the front door.

Dwayne opened it for him, saying "We're gonna be here for a hot minute, so don't think about coming back and starting some mess."

Looking like a ram ready to butt heads with a rival male, Kurt barged past his brother-in-law.

Having to have the last word, Uncle Bubba said, "You heard my nephew. Don't start none, won't be none!" As he closed the door, he crooned, "Bad boys, bad boys, whatcha gonna do? Whatcha gonna do when they come for you?"

Get your copy of *No Right Way to Do a Wrong Thing* today!

POEM: A DAY WITHOUT JESUS

from
POETIC PEACE
by Rose Marie Grandberry

Some tend to think they can live without Jesus in their life.
Perhaps that's the reason for all our trouble and strife.
Our world is filled with many enticing things.
They look good, but think about the trouble they bring.

Oh we'll say, "One time won't hurt to try."
But that's the devil talking and you know it's a lie.
It's his duty to deceive us and make things look good.
He believes that he can do all things, just like Jesus could.

He makes everything seem like the best there is—
until after you try it and your world turns to tears.
Oh let him go on his merry way.
You don't need him to comfort you on any day.

He will continue to come by and knock on your door.
Simply tell him, "I've got Jesus. What do I need you for?"

Jesus is all we ever need.

Let's get on our knees and call on Him.
He'll take us back in spite of any of them.
God knows our hearts from beginning to end.
He is the best One to call when needing a friend.

THE MERRY HEARTS INSPIRATIONAL SERIES . . .

9 780986 314971